GoD SEES ME
all the time

by Denise Vezey
Illustrated by Victoria Ponikvar Frazier

Chariot Victor Publishing
A Division of Cook Communications

Dedicated to:

Our daughter Joy, who was the inspiration for these stories.

Psalm 16:8

Chariot Victor Publishing,
a division of Cook Communications, Colorado Springs, Colorado 80918
Cook Communications, Paris, Ontario
Kingsway Communications, Eastbourne, England

GOD SEES ME ALL THE TIME

The song, "I'll Be a Sunbeam," quoted on page 22, was written by Nellie Talbout and is now in public domain. The music was written by Edwin O. Excell.

Printed in Canada
03 02 01   5 4 3 2

Designed by Art Attack Creative, Inc.
Illustrations by Victoria Ponikvar Frazier

ISBN 0-78143-087-9

Library of Congress Cataloging-in-Publication Data

Vezey, Denise
    God sees me all the time / by Denise Vezey ; illustrated by Victoria Ponikvar Frazier.
        p. cm. -- (Getting to know God series)
        Summary: Through several real life experiences a little girl learns that no matter where she is or what she does God sees her and watches over her.
        ISBN 0-7814-3087-9
        [1. God--Fiction. 2. Christian life--Fiction.] I. Frazier, Victoria   Ponikvar, 1966- ill. II. Title.
    III. Series.PZ7.V627Go 1999
    [E]--dc21

                                                                                98-46427
                                                                                    CIP
                                                                                    AC

Table of Contents

1 My tummy wants a cookie   4

2 My secret place   13

3 my reward   22

My tummy wants a cookie

Mommy is busy baking
the cookies I like best.
"Oh, Mommy,
can I pleeease have one?"

She smiles at me.
"These are for dessert, honey.
Let's wait until after dinner."

I spy, I sneak, I sniff.
Quick—I take a whiff!

What can it hurt?
No one is looking.
Mommy said, "No,"
but my tummy wants a cookie!

I say "hello" to my puppy, Peaches.
I pet his face and give him kisses.
Then, I swing high in the sky,
and touch the clouds with my toes.

All of this makes a little girl very hungry.

I peek through the kitchen window.
Mommy is at the front door.

I go back in and am all alone—
alone with the yummy cookies.

My fingers tip-toe across the plate.
I take the cookie with the most candy,
and gently push all the others back into place.
Mommy won't even see one is gone!
Quick, here she comes!

Mommy bakes more cookies.

She says, "Some people think if nobody is around,

you can do something bad and no one will know.

But God sees us all the time."

All of a sudden, my tummy feels funny.

Does Mommy know I took a cookie?

Even if she doesn't, God sees me.

I run to Mommy

and throw my arms around her.

"I'm sorry, Mommy.

I took a cookie when you were at the door.

Only one bite is missing."

She pats my head and says,

"I forgive you."

We kiss, we hug, we smile.
We talk for just awhile.

Now that I know
God's always looking,
I'll wait like I'm told,
if my tummy wants a cookie.

My secret place

My friends and I like to play hide and seek.

Do you?

When we play,

I go to a place no one knows about!

I run, I slip, I slide.
I stop, I scrunch, I hide.

Around the bushes
quickly I race.
Under a huge rock
is my secret place.

We start playing after supper.

I'm it!

I begin to count, one-two-three . . .

ready or not, here I come!

Faster and faster I chase.

When I find everybody,

I am happy.

No one was in my secret place.

Now it's my turn to hide.

I look to make sure no one is following me.

I hike through the tall grass.

I creep under a rock into my hiding place
and wait.

It is dark in here.

No one is calling my name.

I peek out to see if anyone is looking for me.

It is getting dark outside!

Where did the sun go?

Where are my friends?

My heart makes a thump.

I am all alone . . . all alone . . . all alone.

Just last week Daddy told me,

"God always watches over His children.

They are never out of His sight."

I am one of His children because I trust in Him.

Now when my heart thumps, I think

God sees me . . . God sees me . . . God sees me.

I am not alone.
I can be brave.

God is watching me.
He is with me everywhere I go.
I do not have to be scared.

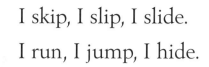

I skip, I slip, I slide.
I run, I jump, I hide.

If I'm hiding and
you can't see my face,
God still sees me
in my secret place.

My reward

I learned a new song!
"A sunbeam, a sunbeam,
Jesus wants me for a sunbeam.
A sunbeam, a sunbeam,
I'll be a sunbeam for Him."

I skip, I swing, I play.
I read, I sing, I pray.

When I get to heaven
and see the Lord,
His words, "Well done, little servant,"
will be my reward.

When I woke up this morning,
my little brother's baseball cap
was under my bed.
I'll put it back in his room
so he can find it.

On the playground,
Mandy Parkins forgot where the bathroom was!
She's only four and a half.

So, I took her hand
and led her the right way.

When I am good and help someone,
it pleases God.
He sees me all the time.
He is always watching me.

Even though I am not grown up,
I can be kind and serve.

Last Friday, I had a bad day.
My dress wasn't pretty,
my hair was a mess,
and I felt grumpy inside.

But Mommy asked me to sweep the floor
and play with my baby sister.
"Oh, Mommy, do I have to?" I asked.
"I don't feel like it."

Then I remember

that God is watching me.

He is right beside me, helping me to be kind to others.

Knowing He is there makes me feel glad inside.

I skip, I swing, I play.
I read, I sing, I pray.

When I get to heaven
and see the Lord,
His words, "Well done, little servant,"
will be my reward.

Thank You, Lord, for watching over me.
You see everything I do and are always with me.
Amen.

You are the God who sees me.
Genesis 16:13, NIV

God Sees Me All the Time

Age: 4-7

Life Issue: My child doesn't understand that God sees us every moment of our day.

Spiritual Building Block: Faith

Learning Styles

Visual Learning Style: Go to a park or shopping mall with your child. Watch how people treat one another and talk about this with your child (mommies/daddies helping children on gym equipment, children sharing toys or working together, someone assisting a senior citizen or carrying drinks to a table at a food court, etc.). Explain how God sees our every action and wants us to treat others with kindness and consideration.

Auditory Style: Look for stories in a Bible storybook that talk about people helping people (Jesus feeding the 5,000 and other miracles, the story of Ruth, Christians in the early church, etc.). Read them to your child. Discuss ways that we can help others. Why is it important not to deliberately hurt people?

Tactile Learning Style: As your family relaxes after a meal, ask your child: "Who is watching you?" Allow the child to name each person in the room. Have the child go to unoccupied room nearby. Ask the same question. When the child returns, talk to him or her about how God sees us when no other person can. Why is it important to choose to do good even if no one sees us?